The People Are America, Sparkle Eyes

and

Fifty-two Other Poems
(1941-2011)

by

David E. Christensen

Author of HEALING THE WORLD (2005)
EARTH IS OVERPOPULATED NOW (2007)
TWO ELEPHANTS IN THE ROOM (2010)
ONGOING LIFE and DNA LOTTERY (2011)
THIS APOCALYPTIC CENTURY (2014)

TABLE OF CONTENTS

PREFACE

Years ago I put together for Carol two notebooks of my poems. Each included about two dozen poems selected from the few hundred I had written over eighty-some years. They were poems she had liked or that I thought she would like. After our fifty six years of happy of marriage, Carol died ten years ago.

Most of the poems in those two notebooks were included in my first poem book, "Ongoing Life, DNA Lottery" (2011) or this one.

To me there is nothing magical about writing poetry. I believe everyone has a poet or artist inside that just needs encouragement to come out, even if only for one's self or their family.

Some might argue that many of mine are not "real poems" at all. Clearly, most of mine are not in the classical rhymed or metered mode. But in our time the old conventions of writing poems apparently have been set aside. And at least no other poem book that I know of has included notes as to a poem's genesis, which may be of interest as history or to those with poetic inclinations.

I had hopes that my four books on critical issues facing the human family (see title page and front cover) would catch the interest of someone who might further those concerns and my deep belief that solutions for the human family can come only with a global government to deal with what obviously are global problems. It hasn't happened so we blindly go on, probably to chaos in our world-wide "civilization" during this century.

I had no illusions that my first poem book or this one would be of general interest. These have been put together for the enjoyment and insight of our four children and six grandchildren, and others who might encounter the books or any of the poems.

D.E.C.

ACKNOWLEDGEMENTS

My first "thank you" for this book's completion must go to my four children, who, after my first book of poems ("Ongoing Life, DNA Lottery," 2011) was published, encouraged me to put together another.

And before thanking two individuals for the completion of this book, I must thank son Dan for years ago converting many of my oldest poems, first onto small disks and much later onto the hard drives of several computers. (I bought my first computer in 1987 at a yard sale for $75.)

Months ago I did start on another poem book, but I encountered many format issues. My son Alan's patient expertise was always there to help this forgetful old man. So thank you, Alan. Without your help I may have abandoned this volume two venture.

Further, difficulties in the publication of my latest book ("This Apocalyptic Century," 2014) discouraged me from undertaking another publishing venture at all. However, Bob Presley offered to help me follow through with a different publisher for this volume. Thanks, Bob, in advance for that to happen smoothly and soon.

Writing poems may be a solitary endeavor, but sharing selected poems in a volume involves a circle of encouraging children and friends. Thank you.
Dave Christensen

CHAPTER ONE

INTRODUCTION

My first book of poems, "Ongoing Life, DNA Lottery" (2011) included forty-six poems in five "chapters" from "Cosmos" and "Religion" to "Whimsy." This poem book, volume two, presents fifty-four poems. And I hope to put together a volume three in 2015 or 2016.

In this second poem book, poems are presented simply in the order in which I wrote them. In that way as one reads along, poems on diverse topics will intermingle and be a surprise as they follow one another. The poems included are from the 1940s to 2011 and touch on most of the topics that are in the first poem book.

Since the poems are in chronological order, the poems themselves and notations about some of them offer insights into my activities, my wide-ranging and changing thoughts and interests, my travels – most of which were made during World War II and with my wife Carol up to the year 2000. Several poems also reflect "current news.

Why do I write poems? Sometimes a poem almost writes itself when an idea, a word or a phrase come to mind. Other times something nags at me and won't go away until a poem or "letter to the editor" emerges. I write poems mostly for myself although I have shared several at various venues. I also have been encouraged by my children and others to share my poems in book form.

My poem-writing style, sometimes metered and rhymed, but usually free verse, is direct. There is no mystical message or coded meaning in any of them. As mentioned in the Introduction to my first poem book, even though a poem was written years before, I retain the "poetic license" to tinker with it, perhaps changing a word here or there, hopefully toward improved clarity. Alphabetical and topical indices of the poems in this book are included at the end.

I hope that through the poems in this book, Carol's and my four children, their spouses, my six grandchildren and others may gain further insight into the interests and mental processes of their Dad, father-in-law, Grandpa,friend, or "this old guy in his nineties."

And I have a suggestion about reading any poem: Do not read any poem hurriedly. Most poems were crafted slowly and thoughtfully! Read each slowly, sensing meter and rhyme if there, letting the message of the words and feelings sink in. Enjoy! And don't move too quickly to another poem.

David E. Christensen   May 2014
(davechris@mchsi.com)
(I welcome comments about the book or any poem.)

CHAPTER TWO – 1940s

Nature

GOLD TATTERS

The trees
    their summer colors shed;
Leaves drifting down,
    earth's winter bed.

Bright leaves,
    by fall's sear slashes gone,
Torn, tattered summer,
    fallen down.

Are once green leaves,
    now withered, brown,
Wistful, wishing
    for a spring again?

October 1941

NEGRO CHILDREN

I saw them,
    Playing barefoot
    Beside the tracks,
    Laughing, dancing,
    Singing...Carefree?

To live and die
    Knowing little beyond
    Their coal-dusted corner
    Of a great city?

Can their world
    Be broadened?
    Are they satisfied,
      for now?
Are their parents?

May 1943

*(I wrote this after seeing Negro children playing
by the tracks in Atlanta on my way to Boca Raton,
Florida. I was on my way to Accra, Gold Coast
(now Ghana), during World War II. These children
were the first Negroes I had really noticed before.
As far as I knew, there were none in West
Elmhurst, IL, Watertown, SD or Mankato, MN;
and I was on my way to a British colony peopled
by Negroes.)*

SEPTEMBER 5, 1939

Ah, life is sweet, but oh, so short!
Seems but this morn I saw a lass,
With friendly smile and "goldie skirt"
Brushing past my startled eyes!

The years have passed with ups and downs,
While she has stayed in mem'ry fast.
Vain secret, mine: she was my life,
In my thoughts from first to last.

Oh, glad sweet morn, my life to tell...
I looked at her and saw her heart,
Then stubbed my heart...and fell!

August 29, 1943

*(Written during World War II at Air Transport
Command Headquarters in Accra, Gold Coast,
where I was stationed. The poem is about my first
days as a freshman at Mankato State Teachers
College in Mankato, Minn. We became engaged in
1944, during World War II, married February
1946 (for 56 years!).)*

GOD AND THE BLIND MEN

God laughs at human selfishness,
For who, but God, holds title
    to this earth, to will its use,
Even to let blind men carve it,
    waste it,
    and build empires,
    one toppling atop another,
For no reason but for self and greed,
    and the hollow glory of the
        empty grasp?

God laughs at petty human selfishness,
    but with an aching heart.
For only He knows the vast and glorious
    empires beyond the horizons
        of destiny,
But to which all men are blind
    until by faith they use the earth
        wisely,
    and work together
        for the common good.

July 9, 1944

BABY WITH A FUTURE?

There he sleeps....
    Bound to his mother's back
      with thrice-mended rags
    Which press tightly her breasts
    And weigh heavily on her bare
      bony shoulders.

He sleeps with rolling head,
    As countless flies
    Cluster about sticky nostrils,
      puss-y closed eyes,
    And dried, half-open mouth.

He sleeps on....
    While his barefoot, ragged,
      half-blind mother
    Taps your sleeve,
    Rattles her peanut tin,
    And presses it to your sleeve
      as she softly asks,
    "Americaine, mohnee for bebby?"

8 September 1945

(Yes, it was like that in downtown Casablanca in (French) Morocco, during World War II. The war and a drought brought many destitute poor people

into the city, and some were always near the Excelsior Hotel where junior officers who worked at the Air Transport Command offices lived. I still get a catch in my throat whenever I read this poem and see the eyes of this pathetic little lady and her baby in rags in my mind's eye.)

CHAPTER THREE – 1950s – 1960s

POINT OF VIEW

A dull day...with smoky fog.
    Trees loom as gaunt skeletons;
    Buildings appear as ghosts.
    Dirty, sooty puddles everywhere,
Sewers clogged by frozen black slush.
A day for indoors...
Away from biting cold
That shivers me down the street
After a tumbling hat.

A misty day...buildings appear
As dim, dream-like forms;
    Trees are shadows...
Each branch jewel-tipped
    With a droplet of crystal.
Cobalt pools and rivulets in melting snow
Make miniature fairylands
That change with the minute.
A crisp day...with bracing air
    That makes one's face tingle...
    So glad to be alive!

February 1951

(Contrasting views of the same
winter day in Chicago.)

SAVANNA

The bush land unfolds for hours
    Below the droning plane.
Mostly tan landscape,
With scattered dull green bushes,
    Flat-topped trees,
And clusters of cone-topped huts
    Simmering in the
        parched vastness.

We fly too high to see the people
    And their cattle,
But I wonder...
    How do they live...
    What are they doing today?...
    Are they happy?

May 1953

(This is about the "savanna," the vast region of Africa that lies between West Africa and the Sahara and between the Sahara and Central Africa. It conveys memories of the many trips I made during World War II across that area-- usually in a DC-3 aircraft--from Accra, along the "Gold Coast", usually with stops in Kano and Maiduguri, Nigeria, El Fasher and El Genina in French Central Africa, and on to Khartoum at the joining of the White and Blue Nile Rivers in Anglo-Egyptian Sudan. Names of nations have changed!)

DUST IN THE SUNLIGHT

Specks of dust
   Churn and drift idly
In a slim shaft of sunlight
   That streams through a crack
      in the door.

Like tiny worlds,
   Each aimlessly alone,
   In a vast universe,
      ...even as you and I?

(Dust in the light shaft,
   Where is your God?)

Perhaps,
   On some cosmic scale,
   Our massive galaxy is but a
      molecule of expanding gas,
   An atom in a rock,
      or a flower,
      or in the leg of a chair
      ...seating a super being!?

(Dust in the sunlight,
   Is your God, OUR God?)

March 1960

GIVE YOURSELF THE PRESENT

Give yourself the present
  --The here and now--
  And find a new world of beauty
    ...overlooked in
    haste and blindness.

Give yourself the present
  And find a new world of friends
    ...unnoticed before
By prejudice or indifference.

Give yourself the present
  And find comfort
  In understanding our bounteous world...
    rich and diverse
    in people and culture,
    each with its unique contribution.

Give yourself the greatest present of all:
  The gift of living to the fullest
    Each moment of the now,
  In the golden fullness of consciousness--
    that separates the dimming past
    from the unfolding future.
      * * *
But, paradox of paradoxes...
  This is a gift no God can bestow:

Living in "the now" is a gift
you alone must give yourself
as you learn to face,
courageously and maturely,
The realities of your own time,
your own place,
your own self.

October 1961

WE SAY...THEY SAY...

We say we are there to defend some of them
        from Communism;
And our "boys"—(boys no longer!)--
        fight and die in leach-infested rice
paddies and in the steaming booby-trapped
jungles and in the streets of Saigon.
More so-called "Communists" are always
        there,
                just as there are more and more of us
                and our engines of war
                with each passing week.

We say we were asked to regain the freedom
        ...of some of them,
Yet our staunchest supporters are those
        who would enrich themselves
        with money and power.
        (Who do the changing string of
                "leaders" represent
                ...but themselves?)

The rising cost of rice eats away
        the meager purse of the peasant,
While the Viet Cong say,
        "Go home colonial aggressors",
        And the prostitute and black marketer
                say, "Stay a little longer,
                Yankee man."

Some patriots say,
  "We must fight there with honor to
  bring freedom
  to an oppressed people."
  "The eyes of the world and our
  soldiers are upon us,
  we cannot turn back,
  we must not fail."
While other patriots ask,
  "Does compounding poor judgment
  enhance a tarnished image?"
  "If this be a just cause do more allies
    rally to our side?...

Or are we ever more alone---
  as we sink deeper into this uicksand?"

Oh, that we could halt this cruel war
  (or is it already too late?)
Before freedom and honor in word and deed
  are corrupted beyond repair
in our own fair land,
  ...and in this once lovely but now
  charred and blood-soaked place.
We must stop this madness
  lest what remains of freedom and
  honor slip beyond the reach
    ...of this generation.

(early 1966)

VIETNAM PERSPECTIVE: 1984?

"War is peace!"
"Ignorance is strength!"
"Freedom is slavery!"

The Vietnam war grows day by bloody
      day...
But never mind, this is a PEACEFUL WAR.
      We bomb and kill and burn
      in this small distant place
      because we are a peace-loving people
      seeking only freedom and peace
      (...for those we destroy.)

[Big Brother sees light at the tunnel's end.]

The credibility gap widens...
      But never mind, IN IGNORANCE
      THERE IS STRENGTH and
      security!
Trust not the ferment of truth-seeking
      in our midst.
Trust only our super-patriotic President
      ...and his generals
      ...and the managed news.

[Big Brother knows what is best for his
      peace-loving people.]

Dissenters to this madness are called
        traitors...
But never mind, TO BELIEVE in our
        Bill of Rights and Freedom
        IS TO BE A SLAVE to old ideas.

    Trust not our heritage of inquiry
        and debate and tolerance;
    Trust instead our Big Brother,
        who expects robot-like acceptance
        of his will.

    [Will 1984 come with tomorrow?
    Is a Big Brother
        watching YOU - NOW?]

May 1967
*(The three quotes at the beginning of this
poem are slogans from George Orwell's book,
"Nineteen Eighty Four," published in 1949. The
quotes and this poem are eerily prescient of our
misguided struggles in Iraq and Afghanistan.)*

CHAPTER FOUR – 1970s

FREEDOM?

Like a mirage
   is the search for
   individual freedom.

The hermit is not free.
   He simply denies
   humanity by his isolation.

Freedom is elusive as smoke,
   and can be appreciated
   only with others;

And with others
   it must be balanced with
   limits and responsibilities.

   *   *   *

Thus "freedom" is a paradox:
If one is alone "freedom" is useless.
It has meaning only when
   compromised – with others!

1970

THE PEOPLE ARE AMERICA!

Not ribbons of concrete and tar
    rumbling with wheeled brutes
    of steel, plastic and glass,
Not whirling dynamos and black,
    belching smokestacks,
    Not crowded ghettoes
        or miles of boxes
            where more people live,
Not purple mountains and fruited plains
    or once clear streams
    and golden beaches....

WE ARE AMERICA!

Not great marble monuments
    on the eastern shore,
    Or domed and columned structures
    in fifty capital cities,
Not our red, white striped flag
    with fifty bright stars on blue...

NO, WE ARE AMERICA!

We are sons and daughters of pioneers
    who struggled to America's shores
    from far-off places of poverty
    and oppression.

We are progeny of brave revolutionaries
    who brought forth with this nation
    a new hope for mankind!
We are children of those with red skin
    who were here before and were
    cheated of their heritage.
We are children of those
    torn from homes in Africa
    and dragged to this land as slaves.

We are children of those who came from
    Europe and China in hope and built
    railroads, bridges and homes.
Yes: Children of all who were here
    before
    and the hopeful immigrant of
    yesterday,

WE ARE AMERICA!

Should we, like monarchs of old,
    hide behind our comforts,
    leaving America a dream half-
    fulfilled?
Shall dreams be forgotten,
    as rewards heap on those who exploit
    their brothers and sisters
    and this once lovely land?

Can we let our eyes see
    unfairness and oppression

burgeoning in our midst?
Can we unchain those who cry out
    to open our eyes and hearts?

THE PEOPLE ARE AMERICA!

Come, good people,
    bind each other's wounds.
    Together let us make dreams
    come true for ourselves
And help our brothers and sisters here
    And around this bounteous planet!

Feb. 1970

THREADS OF CONSCIOUSNESS

Threads of consciousness
    Spin out a web that is my life...
Linking past with present,
    Place with place,
        new friends with old.

The web is ever-expanding...
    Probing and filling outer
        and inner spaces,
Bonded by flimsy filaments
    To the "real world"...
        that isn't there!

* * * *

My world
    ...and the worlds of all others
    Are real only as perceived
        through personal and unique
Threads of consciousness
    And airy webs of memory,
        As minds go on spinning...
            Spinning...
                spinning...

October 1971

NEW BEGINNINGS

Winter's sear bite and long shadows
  have passed.
Birds take over leafless trees
  with cheery chirp
  and expectant chatter.
Dull, brown hillsides come alive
  with a pale green glow
  as tender shoots spring
  from moist dark earth.
Spring is a greening, warming world
  of new beginnings!

Put away muffler and boot
  for short sleeve and suntime!
Spring is a time to reflect, to renew,
  to clear dust from house
  and cobwebs from mind,
Each day for new growth,
  new fulfillment.
   * * *
Each spring begins a new cycle of life
  --as fresh and hopeful
  as all that have gone before.
Each season has its own glory:
  "spring" is for "new beginnings"!

April 1972

(Written for Dave and Eve McIntosh and for an Easter morning sunrise get-together on their lovely hilltop south of Carbondale.)

PLAY BALL!

Batter up!
Pitch it over...Strike one...
    Ball one....
    A slow wind-up...and....a...
    Line drive to center!

Batter up with a man on first!
Strike one...Here comes the next one...
    Bouncing ball to short...
    Quick throw to second, one out,
    And to first...double play!

Great play...team play...
Great game...sportsmanship....
    Fun game...America's game...
    "Boys of summer"...Idols all!
       * * *
Play ball?
No batter up.
    No high-stepping wind up.
    No strike one...or two...
    No...all strike out!

Fun game?...No...money game.
Workers all...businessmen all...
    Strike, haggle, strike.

Tarnished idols;
   Baseball is big business.

Stadiums silent;
   Stadiums empty;
   All players out,
   Everyone is out.

   *   *   *

"Work-up" or "sides"?...
Toss the bat..."Crows feet!"...
Kick the bat..."We'll take "outs"!
Back to street and sand lot
Where it all began...for fun!

April 1972

*(During baseball players' strike and
remembering our playing softball on
the empty lots next door to 567 Saylor
Ave.,Elmhurst, IL, my home. A neighbor-
hood men's 16 inch fast softball team
also had their diamond, backstop,
bleachers in the empty field across from
the houses on Saylor Avenue. (One summer
I, with flour and water "paint," painted
numbers on the scoreboard squares after
each half-inning.)*

OUR MOTHER

Carrie Elsie Olga Loken,
        born on April 5, 1890,
        to coal merchant (and former
Wisconsin farmer) Ole and
        midwife Anna,
Youngest of seven, most of whom
        did not survive to grow up.
As teenager she learned to drive
        the only car in the neighborhood.
She became high school teacher of
        Norwegian and school principal.

Lovely face and lovely eyes....
        of "Little Woman"....
Whose beauty and softness enchanted
        neighbor Emun Christensen,
        a young soldier going off to war.

Loving heart and mind....
        whose gentleness and keenness
        as mother and teacher
        helped mold young minds,
Who sought to see behind words....
        and into the heart....
        of a seeking child.

Loving hands....
        whose warm touch soothed
        the sick and frightened,
Whose labors and caresses spoke
        so clearly a language
        more powerful than words.

Loving arms....
        that enfolded four infants,
        children, teenagers
        and grown-up children,
Whose strength overcame lean years
        and the sweaty toil of
        homemaking.

Loving soul....
        Whose patience and faith,
        through depression years of
        poverty,
        and years of sickness and pain,
Kindled a quiet respect and love
        in those who came to know her.

*   *   *

Let all rejoice who loved her
Rejoice in comforting memories
        of a rich and loving life,
While we yet enjoy a fullness of
        breath and while daylight

still sparkles in our eyes!
We love you, our Mother, rest in peace.

March 1973

*(I wish I had long conversations with
my Mom about "life" and her memories,
but somehow I didn't talk much about
those things with her. Finally, she
was in a Fort Scott, Kansas, nursing
home after several weeks of hospital-
ization during which prescriptions [for
diabetes, arthritis and heart condition]
were re-stabilized. She died suddenly on
January 10, 1973 at 82 years of age
after a brief bout with the flu and
pneumonia. She is buried in the Crystal
Lake Cemetery on North Penn Avenue
in Minneapolis in the Loken family plot
and near the Christensen plot.)*

ENERGY CRISIS?

Energy crisis?....to hell!
Bot my rod to do a hundred - flat out--
    and she'll do it,
      troopers or no troopers!
No one kin tell me to hold her to 50 -
    or stay home Sundays!

This country moves on wheels, man;
    ain't nobody,
    from the lyin' president
    to them A-rabs
Kin stop my wheels from turnin'!

        *   *   *

Or kin they?
What if gas gits to a dollar a gallon;
Or taxes on my beast go to a hundred,
    Then mebbe I'd hafta cool it.

But cheez....
    How kin I feel like me....
     like a man....like an American
.....To hafta carpool or go slow
    or bike around.....or walk?

      November 1973

*(The "dollar" and "hundred" are like
ancient history....And today's prices
will keep going up!)*

TO A DAY LILY STALK

Blossom fair...now spent...

Such stately charm
Your long and slender stalk implies,
 Head high above all around.

Perchance a graceful golden crown
Was your living glory,
With touch of pink,
Petals edged in bronze...
         ravishing...breathtaking...
With dainty necklace green...
         but...
Blossom fair,
Did your beauty come and go...unseen?
And what is beauty
         Without the seeing?

                *   *   *   *

 You are what you are,
We are what we are;
         life is what it is.
You will live on
         in other gold-crowned lilies –
And your beauty, seen or unseen,
         Can only in a mind live on.

                              August 1974

TOPLESS?

With a joggle and a jiggle
As up and down they bounce,
   Male blood runs hot!

With a wiggle and a waggle
As 'round and round' they jounce
   Men's eyes pop out!

With her joggles and men's ogles,
Her act you might denounce,
   But "topless" she's not!

December 1974

*(A possible word contradiction brought to
mind by Carbondale's first "topless"
go-go girl bar that opened on East Walnut
in November 1974, and by a scene from
"The Graduate" movie.)*

I LOVE YOU

A sparkling twinge
when you suddenly appear,
A catch of breath
to hear your voice,
A warmth of heart
when you are near,
To be with you always
is my choice.

A pleasant glow
when eye meets eye,
Chills course spine
if fingers touch,
A lump in throat
when we say goodbye;
My sweet,
I love you so very much!

January 1975

"CHRISTY" IS MY DAD

Born April 8, 1890
     in Lanesboro, Minnesota,
seventh of eight children of
     Anna and John, a cooper...

Who as a youth was molded
     by Sister Ann, the Olson farm,
     North Star Foundry, South
     High, Ann Fish, and pre-med
     courses at the U of M,

Who was awed by the sparkle of the
     stars, the power of a tornado,
     the mystery of fire, the beauty
     and miracle of nature and
     the loveliness of Carrie,
     the girl next door,

Who was incensed by the folly and
     wastage of war and the
     inhumanity of prejudice;
Who was inspired by the teachings of
     Jesus, Kagawa, Gandhi and the
     Reverend King, and used
     Grenfell, Livingstone and
     Pasteur as names for three sons,

Who spent working years
      at the "Yumca" in Ashland, South
      Chicago's Sears Y" in South Chicago,
      the Watertown Youth Center, and
      Fort Scott,
      --Always ready with song or story--
      --Always ready to help someone,
         and left a lasting imprint on
      those who camped at Namakagon,
      Hastings and Watymca,

Who shared fifty-four married years with
Carrie, the lovely next door Loken girl
      as they raised Edward, David, Alan
      and Dorothy Ann
Through days of the "Roaring Elgin", ulcers,
      Fuller Brushes, collecting meager
      pledges, drawing strength from
      Watertown friends—Doctor Freeburg,
      Betty Thompson, Hazel Haggarty and
      Floyd Perkins.

And even with Carrie gone and eyes failing,
      Planted a tree so those who come later
      may enjoy,
Who always explored the heart of mankind
      and the vastness and glory of the
      universe....in his mind,
    And willed his body for medical research?

xy   xy   xy

All these and more
          are Emun Peter Christensen,
Known to many as "Christy",
          I'm proud he's "Dad" to me!

                              May 1975

(Dad died in a DesMoines, Iowa, nursing home on June 16,1975. He was 85 years old. After his body was used by fledgling doctors for two years, his ashes were finally laid to rest at the University of Iowa Medical School section of Oakland Cemetery in Iowa City on June 10,1977.)

CAMPFIRE

Dusk falls gently
As colors slip to shades of gray
As the mantle of the dark
Settles ever closer.

The campfire's flames
Leap from burning embers,
And probe the deepening dark
With flickering orange shafts
That pierce the veil of darkness
And create ghostly dancing shadows.

The play between dark and light
Is like life's constant battle
Between the comfort of the visible
And the known
And the mystery and danger
Of the unknown.

October 1977

FORGOTTEN NIGHT

Trains a-huffing, bells a-ringing,
Horns a-blowing, trucks a-screeching,
Buses too, mezzuin chanting,
Crows a-cawing, cocks a-crowing...

In that order or some other
May just give one's sleep disorder.
May just make one toss, turn over,
Plug up ears, hide under cover!

*   *   *

Bright rays of sun, "new day dawnin."
A smile, some tea, the night forgotten.

May 1979

*(At 56 Miller's Road, Bensontown,
Bangalore, in southern India, I spent a couple of
weeks in 1979. And it happened, just like that for
several nights there.)*

GREEN HAIR

I saw a man with cropped green hair,
now green is color ordinar,
      So why my turn?
      Why my stare?

Gentle color grass and leaf,
chlorophyll magic beyond belief,
      Feathers green and fish sometimes
      ...but hair?

      If green hair was caused
      By diet vegetarian,
      In India this phenomenon
      should be the common one.

              May 1979

THE SPIRITS OF CHRISTMAS

The spirit of Christmas is like a wreath...
　　whose circle represents the never-ending
　　cycle of birth, living and dying of all things
　　　　on our bounteous jewel in space.

The spirit of Christmas is like a Christmas
　　tree whose lights put sparkles of joy
　　in the eyes and hearts of all, whose
　　decorations bring memories
　　　　of Christmases long gone.

The spirit of Christmas is like a candle...
　　whose gentle light, like Bethlehem's star,
　　represents the love of family and friends,
　　and pushes back shadows of loneliness.

The spirit of Christmas is like Santa Claus...
　　legendary symbol of wonder and laughter
　　And...m y s t e r y...in unopened gifts
　　and giving of oneself for others.

The spirit of Christmas is like a Christmas
　　Carol and a Christmas bell that sings forth
　　and rings forth with clarity,
　　"Peace on Earth, Goodwill to All!"

But most of all, the spirit of Christmas
    is the spirit of baby Jesus and all children,
    As symbols of love, new beginnings and
    hope for the human family.

                December 1979

CHAPTER FIVE – 1980s

Travel/ Record

WILIKE MORNING

In early dawn smoke rises gently from
thatched huts and tin-roofed resettlement
         homes.
Cries of infants and coughs that broke the
night's stillness are past.
The staccato of gunfire that punctuated the
night with instant terror is done;
And the symphony of the roosters is over.

Smokes merge with the rising mist of the
stillness.
Already with first light, asentimiento homes
are alive with murmurs and clatter;
Chickens peck and chatter among puddles
and mud; a pig grunts her way through the
sticky red mass;

Booted, green-clad militia--some so very
young--slog up the hill to take a turn at
watch;
Riders maneuver nimble horses up and
down the slick slopes to get on with chores.
And barefooted children, wide-eyed and
beautifully curious, ignore the mud as they
come to visit again with strangers from their

too-powerful northern neighbor.

Always the children!
Nicaragua's--and the world's--
hope for a better future
is in their open minds,
their strong hands and hearts!

July 1985

*(Wilike Asentimiento, Zelaya, Nicaragua, is an
 agricultural cooperative community designed for
one hundred families. It was organized in the
 interior of Nicaragua by the government in
February 1985. By mid-July about 65 families,
 harassed by U.S. supported "Contras" attacking
individual farms in this isolated area, had moved
to Wilike for security and were struggling to make
a new life in the raw landscape. Our "Witness for
Peace" group spent several days there.)*

THE DRAGON'S NEW COAT

The dragon's earlier coats,
    Gold, purple and green,
Were torn asunder
    Amid lightning and thunder
By sword-like teeth and talons.

The dragon now has a new coat of
    red.
    But how loose should it be
    For easy movement, and yet.....
    To protect a tender belly
From razored swords?

Is the dragon happy in its new red coat
    With yellow design?
Would a striped coat of red and green
    Be more comfortable and
More pleasing to the dragon's eye?

The dragon is not asleep.
    It moves slowly...lazily.....
While it watches...stretches.....
    With one talon clutching
    scraps
    .....Of the old coats.

April 1987

(I wrote THE DRAGON'S NEW COAT when Carol and I were visiting Shanghai in April 1987 after teaching near Zhengzhou, China, for two months. It suggests what we saw and learned: That even though the Communist Party and machine [the "red" coat] dominate China's large and small and small cities [less so the countryside], there was considerable dissatisfaction toward the authoritarian and inefficient regime and wishes for more individual freedom. The red and green "striped coat" suggests a mixed economy, similar to India's blend of socialism and capitalism under a democratic system, might be workable in China. My allusion to "scraps of old coats" notes that a strong legacy remains in China of feudal days of "purple and gold coated" emperors and of capitalism, the "green coat.")

CHINA 1987

Straining shoulder in stretched harness
    the small muscular ragged worker
    sweats his cart load of concrete beams
    along the green-arched road,
    enduring ear-piercing pig-squeals,
    two-toned blasts from curtained sedans
    and careening, weaving trucks,
    as he plods, kilometer after kilometer,
    six hours back-breaking toil for 7 yuan.

Head in hands,
    the graduate student speaks hopelessly
    of crowded and dirty living quarters,
    a noodle-dominated diet,
    a poorly managed program
    and now a desired position offered
    but for which he will not be released
    by his university.

Ping-pong paddle in hand,
    the young "worker" spends his time
    in games and music,
    earning a salary and living comfortably,
    but doing little as he,
    as so many others,
    use the system's poor management
    for a life of ease.

Hour after dusty hour,
    just as with wheat two weeks ago,
    the wiry farmer spreads his soybeans
    across the road
    to be threshed under the pounding tires
    on wheels large and small,
    then to be winnowed and reformed
    and finally golden beans
    are scooped into bags to fulfill
    a contract with the commune...
    and perchance have some left over
    to sell on open market?

Straining shoulder to shoulder
    in stretched harnesses,
    a pair of workers, horseless,
    pulls an ancient three-row seeder,
    as once again the cycle of
    planting, growing, living and dying
    goes 'round again.

But where is the Glorious New China?
    and to what future?

                        September 1987

*(Dour observations from Carol's and my first
weeks of the second teaching term at Huanghe
University near Zhengzhou, Henan, China. In the
late 1980s 7 yuan would be worth about one US
dollar, and then the worker would have to push the*

cart back to Zhengzhou to push a load the next day. To the amazement and amusement of those around, I got "in harness" on one of our walks and helped [briefly] pull the seeder mentioned in the next to last "Straining shoulder...." stanza.)

CHAPTER SIX – 1990s

War

CHESS GAME

Ivory and ebony pawns face off
Across a squared frontline,
As Kings stand tall on opposite edges
 Of the checkered field.

When and how far pawns to move,
And how the Queen's great power to prove?
When to use rook's power square
Or bishop moving angular?

How best to use the knight's surprise
And when to make a sacrifice?

*   *   *

Options diplomatic fall away
As the real "game" takes the day.
No talks here; kings are blunt!
Kings threaten; kings taunt!

Then, with attack intended
Or provocation mistaken,
Like so many times of old,
Blood, machines and gold
Are sacrificed at the king's command,
 In Persian waters and fields of sand.

October 1990

(Suggesting the pathetic situation of President Bush insisting on S. Hussein's unconditional departure from Kuwait before they could talk about anything, and Bush's out-of-hand rejection of all of Saddam Hussein's suggestions for talks and negotiation to seek ways to end the Persian Gulf confrontation.)

GHOST SHIP

In twilight late a specter eerie
    Moves across the star-splashed sky.
Dim lights in rows a vortex form:
    Seven on sides, in front just one.

With vortex form, no airplane this,
    A ghostly spaceship passing by.
Swift and straight the ship moves on...
    And to the night is lost too soon.

*   *   *

Though specter happened as I say,
    The "Ghost Ship" is my fantasy.
In truth the "window" lines vortexing
    Are light from far below reflecting
Breasts of geese that fly so high,
    In "V" of perfect symmetry.

November 5, 1990

(It happened just like that on the evening of October 28 when Carol and were walking near the Elementary School in Kenyon, Minnesota (Built on Land donated by Carol's grandparents.) A few honks from the geese had alerted us to look high to the east where we saw the "Ghost Ship" (Light from their breasts reflecting was from Kenyon's downtown.)

PLEDGE OF ALLEGIANCE: REVISED

I pledge allegiance to the CONSTITUTION
of the United States of America and to the
Republic it undergirds. Our nation, indivisible,
striving for liberty and justice for all.

[Our nation, one of the United Nations, seeking
a better life for all as we protect our Earth, on
which we all depend.]

January 1991

*(I've never been comfortable pledging
allegiance to and saluting a piece of cloth,
regardless of its presumed symbolism. I am
comfortable substituting the word "CONSTITU-
TION" [and its amendments] in place of the word
"flag" as I say the pledge and stand before the
flag. I am reminded too much of the William Tell
story. I also have changed the words "with liberty
and justice for all" to "STRIVING" for liberty and
justice for all," which, hopefully, is what we are
trying to do. I've deleted the words "under God"
to be consistent with our separation of church and
state.)*
*[At the end, in brackets, is a line that
acknowledges the reality of our global situation,
even though I do not say it in a group reciting the
"Pledge."].*

OF, BY AND FOR THE FEW

From oh so young we are schooled
    That, hand in hand,
    Capitalism and democracy
    Made our country
    Great and good and powerful.

Little note is made of
    The treasures in our good Earth,
    The imported traditions
    Or the hard work and tolerance
    Of most who came to these shores.

Little thought is given to the antithesis
    Between raw capitalism,
    That owns the fourth estate,
    And government of, by and for all people,
    Who depend on the fourth estate for
    TRUTH!

Little note is made
    Of the interdependent web of control
    Among the government's many branches,
    Our economy, the military industry,
    And that fourth estate.

Capitalism was born with the blessing of
    kings, who granted privilege
    And opportunity to the few,

And whose greed for wealth and power
Squeezed peasants to the limit.

Unbridled capitalism, even without kings,
　　Squeezes the struggling many and
　　Heaps great wealth on the few.
　　Great wealth leads to power for the few,
　　And great power leads to tightening control
　　by the few.

Manipulation and squeezing of the masses
　　Leads to a face of democracy,
　　The head of a despot,
　　No heart or voice for the masses,
　　And still greater power and wealth
　　for the few.

Though it may be wrested from kings by blood
　　Or granted by kings against a wall,
　　Democracy is a fragile flower
　　That survives only on the flow of truth
　　And trust among its people.

Democracy matures and blossoms only
　　In a balancing of freedoms
　　with responsibilities,
　　In a striving for the well-being of all
　　...and the good earth.

A democracy withers when used by elites.
　　Then governments of the people,
　　By the people, and for the people
　　Become shams, filled with hollow dreams

...and, under the yoke, slip into history.

A greedy capitalism,
  Like a rampant rogue elephant,
  Will destroy those who feed it.
      So...bridle the pachyderm
      ...and let democracy flourish!

  March 1992

  (Putting together troubling thoughts
  from Reagan and Bush years.)

WASHINGTON AFTER HOURS

See "Washington After Hours"!
   "'Old Town Trolley'
   unlocks the mysteries as
   you enjoy sights and sounds!
"In awe admire brightly illumined
   monuments and memorials:
   The Washington Obelisk,
   The Lincoln and Jefferson Temples,
   The White House, the Capitol,
   The Treasury Parthenon,
   The Kennedy Center.
"Hear the history
   as the trolley rolls,
   sprinkled with ghostly lore.
"You haven't seen Washington until
   you've seen it at night!
   Only twenty dollars."

See "Washington After Hours"!
   "Walk downtown streets
   and in the parks.
"See 'The Other Washington':
   Trash bins overflowing,
   Big and little stores
    'going out of business',
   A bag lady camped
    in Franklin Park,

Men sleeping by many buildings
or under plastic in Lafayette Park
with all their earthly possessions
(across from the White House!),
And see a fat, black rat
scurry under a bush.
"You haven't seen Washington until
you've seen it at night!
No charge...walk it yourself."

November 2, 1995

*(During a few days in Washington
for an AARP workshop, I had the
opportunity to ride the "Old Town
Trolley" one evening and on other
evenings to walk to the east,
northeast, north and northwest of
the Hotel Washington downtown.)*

TIT OR TAT?

Did Katushas provoke an Israel tat?
Or did an Israel tit raise a Hezbollah tat?
By "surgical strikes"
That so tragic-ly strayed,
Now dozens more refugees....dead.

Despite UN resolution
And world condemnation,
Lebanese land Israel occupies ...
While the Hezbollah terrorize ...
But it is the innocent who still dies.

Around the world, what's a tit or a tat?
And how far back should one go for all that?
Is it hopeless? Will wars never end?
Only when grown-up boys set war toys aside
And become thinking, caring,
                              compromising men.

April 1996

*(For decades Israel has continued
its occupation of southern Lebanon
-- "to protect Israel's north" -- in
opposition to UN resolutions but
apparently with the approval of the U.S.
The Hezbollah is always there as a nettle*

against Israeli occupation - and under-standably so. There have been repeated incidents in a "tit for tat" manner, with Israel still occupying Lebanese land, although there is no way to go back to an original tat or tit incident.)

IN WHOSE IMAGE?

God - an old man
With flowing beard and robe?
Benevolent, with power unlimited,
Watching every living thing?

What was God's image
Before life bloomed on Earth,
When dinosaurs dominated,
Before humans evolved?

Did God "make man" in his image?
Or did ignorant, nature-stressed man
Imagine a vengeful or benevolent God
in man's image?

July 1996

FAIRYLAND FLIGHT

With a crescendoing roar
    the lionene engines lift us
Over a carnival of pale green and amber
    flickerings among trees and houses,
With streams of red and white lights
    moving hither and yon all around.

We climb and multi-colored streams and
Points shimmer here and there in the
    blackness,
Only to slip away in the distance
    as soft darkness encloses all.

The half-moon eerily reflects on a wing,
    and I look up
To the moon's brightness
    and the star spangled firmament.

Too soon we touch the ground,
    taxi slowly and park,
And the engines, like two tired lions,
    slowly growl to sleeping silence.

September 1996

*(It happened like this on an evening flight
from St. Louis to the Marion airport. At the*

end of the flight, as we were deplaning, I noted
that after the ignition was cut off the engines
sounded like lions slowly growling and grumbling
themselves to sleep.)

DANCING WITH A BEE

Ask yellow-black demon who attacked David,
    "Why?",
As Dave worked away clearing plant debris?

Right through leather glove, and not just by whim,
The bee stung him, leaving stinger within him!

Dave beat bee away as the wound he sucked
    briefly;
Bee came right back to attack in a fury!

At loss of his stinger was bee angry with him?
Or angered was bee when Dave cleared out bee's
    home?

Regardless the reason for bee's wild attack,
What happened then was a wild fight back!

So rarely is seen such a dance as ensued,
A dance to strike back; a dance in black mood!

With gyrations, slapping, dance steps unheard of
David swung out wildly with hand and with glove

Against monster-mini who had in its mind
To nip at Dave's neck, ears, bald head or behind!

Jumping this way and that with no real precision,

Dave tried to keep bee from further incision!

For minutes the battle in near silence went on,
The buzzer against a hard-breathing old man.

Dave finally able to open garage door;
Flying inside he plopped down on the floor,

To recover composure and a bit of his breath
From the yellow-black demon, intent on his death!

August 1998 *(I was 77 at the time.)*

CHAPTER SEVEN – 2000s

COMMON SENSE TELLS US...

Fair-minded observation informs us that
We live in a world of "haves and have-nots",
A bipolar world, a world bogged down
With deep-seated hates and greed.

Common sense tells us we cannot
Right the wrongs of the past.
There is no way to make right the Inquisition,
The Crusades, pogroms or Holocausts.

The dead cannot be brought back to life;
Disputed ancient boundaries cannot be fixed;
Old battles lost in antiquity cannot be refought;
Refugees cannot all be resettled.

Common sense should tell us that a violent world,
One-fourth rich and three-fourths poor,
Cannot prepare a peaceful and fair future
For the next generations.

Common sense informs us that
A bipolar world filled with hate and greed
Is no seedbed for generations who must learn
To live in peace with sharing.

Common sense tells us, as difficult as it will be,
That grownups must set aside

Bitter, hate-filled learnings from their past
And adopt a new way – for their children.

A new century and millennium is the time
To start anew to give all children a chance
To grow up without fear of death
Or bitter baggage from the past.

Common sense should tell us that:
Hate and greed cannot win a peaceful world;
Hate and greed cannot win a world of justice;
Hate and greed breed more hate and greed.

The time for common sense is now.....
        For our children.
                                        May 2000

        *(A free verse version of key points I
        sent to a number of U.S. and world
        leaders a year ago..... with only one
        response.)*

SPARKLE EYES

Sparkle eyes,
You almost look your age,
As a light snow finally
Bedecks your crown.

Your smile still kindles my heart
And your warm hand on my elbow
Carries silent messages
Of our six decades of love.

October 2000

(I wrote this while Carol and I were at Mayo Clinic, she to learn how to inject herself with insulin to better control her diabetes, I to look into prostate gland issues..)

AMAZING LOVE

Amazing love and questing power
Have brought this lonely soul
Into the fold of Fellowship
Thus making my life whole.

With questions in my mind for years
I've wandered all alone.
This Fellowship of kindred souls
Is now my second home.

Together we find inner peace
And help our world to be
A better place for every one,
A place where all are free.

A place where all are welcomed in,
And all can feel at home.
Where caring true comes from the heart
Until our work is done.

January 2001

*(Alternative and more UU-
friendly words to the familiar
traditional religious song.)*

THOU SHALT NOT KILL

Ignoring Seventh Commandment
And perhaps following Ecclesiastes three,
WE taught him to hate and kill,
And he learned it well.
With excellent performance
          in "Desert Storm,"
A decorated hero, he came home.

But hate grew in a mind askew,
And the hate-skewed mind
Saw only inept government
Trampling freedoms.
So, blinded by hate
He blew away one-hundred sixty eight.

Tomorrow we will kill him
In ceremony "humane."
The Seventh Commandment?
Ecclesiastes three?
We taught him to hate and kill,
And, yes, he learned it well.

June 2001

*(I wrote this the day before Timothy McVeigh
was executed in Terra Haute, IN, for bombing
the Federal Building in Oklahoma City in*

April 1995. I have never been comfortable with
Ecclesiastes 3, verses 3 ("a time to kill"),
and 8 ("a time to hate"). Why should war, hate
and killing be acceptable when the state says
so, contradicting the Seventh Commandment and
what common morality informs us?)

MONGOOSE AND COBRA?

Israel and the Palestinians,
Like mongoose and cobra,
Strike blindly at each other ---
Because each is blind.

Israeli military, police
and bulldozers on one side,
Suicide bombers and stone throwers
On the other.

Long gone from memory
Is the question "who struck first"?
Now it is "tit for tat" and "tat for tit"
In never-ending conflict.

An "eye for an eye' and
"Tooth for a tooth"
Has left both adversaries
Blind, toothless --- and dumb.

Blind to the futility
Of never-ending "retaliations";
Toothless because a watching world
Would not condone all-out war;

And dumb because
Each is held hostage behind

71

Home-grown fanatics and extremists
Who eschew fair talk and solution.

Oh, Israel! Oh, Palestinians!
Abandon mindless "tit for tat" tactics!
Embrace the best in your religions!
And live this new century – in peace!

August 11, 2001

*(For almost a year the mindless "tit for tat"
hostilities have continued and escalated,
with Israel's military on one side against
individuals beyond Arafat's control on the
other. Neither leader is strong enough
politically to move decisively toward a
peaceful solution, and blind support of the
United States' fuels Israel's fire.)*

MOMENTS OF PEACE

Four young deer, none with Bambi spots,
Browse a shadowed wood's edge.
The largest, ears perked high, looks
    directly at me.
I whistle, none move, one tall ear twitches.

High overhead, almost among feathery
    clouds,
A pure white heron leisurely wings the sky.
Across the pond on distant green hill
    sheep browse.
Above our heads hummingbirds dart and
Whir back and forth from sweet dispensary.

Treasured conversation
About cabbages and "would be kings"
Adds to beauty and tranquility.

October 2006

(View from Pat's deck)

THE CHILDREN'S DREAM OF PEACE

It came one night
To the children,
All children around the world,
As a dream, a dream of peace.

How did it come?
Where did it come from?
Who knows?
From a simple prayer?
A simultaneous flash of inspiration?

Each child awoke with questions:
Why do they teach us to hate?
Why do we fight?
Why do we kill each other?
And if we can't all be friends
Can't we get along
Without killing, without hate,
Without taking advantage
          of each other?

Each child also awoke
With an idea:
Why can't the world

Have a day with no one
Harming another person?
Why can't the world have a day
When everyone shares with others,
When everyone helps someone else?

All of the children
Took their questions
And those ideas
And planted them
In the minds
And hearts
Of their parents
And all grownups.

And grownups thought:
"A foolish idea, of course!
But why not try it for one day?"
Each grownup in his or her heart,
Each in his or her mind decides
And encourages others
To open their minds and hearts –
For just one day.

"Old hatreds will not be resolved
By looking only to the past.
But why not set aside
Old hatreds and anger for a day?
Why not try acceptance
And helpfulness
And fairness for just one day?"

And it is agreed.

So a "day of peace" comes to be.
Hour by hour,
As the world turns,
Peace comes as manna,
First in each heart
And each family,
Then on each farm, in each village
Each town, each city.

Guns remain silent;
All weapons idled, drones grounded,
As hour by hour peace and friendship
Blossom to a peace-hungry,
Waiting humanity.......And then,
It comes as a jolt of the obvious:
If we can live in peace for one day,
Why not another, and yet another?
Let the children's dream of peace
Become reality!

All children need a peaceful world
With no fear of ever growing up,
A world of peace for their happiness,
A world of peace for their fulfillment!
A naive dream
From dreamy-eyed children? Perhaps.

But do we grownups have a better plan?
Hate and violence and

The greedy business of war
Are leading to our destruction.
To have peace and fairness and justice
Is always up to grownups.
To have peace or not –

Is up to us.

                                    July 2000
(And the basic theme of this poem did
come in a dream!)

WHERE ARE THEY?

Where are those
Whose parents and grandparents,
Brothers and sisters,
Friends and neighbors
Were incinerated
By a dastardly government –
And mesmerized citizens?

Where are
The hearts of those who
Survived the Holocaust
To start life anew
In a faraway place,
A place called Israel.

Do they not remember
The millions of their
Blood and religion
Snuffed out
By the inhumane regime?

Have they no feelings
For another people
Whose towns and lands,
Orchards and farms were wrested
To create the survivors' homeland?

Is there no heart for refugees,

Living for decades
At the hands of Holocaust survivors,
In a living hell called "Gaza"?

Of all the world's people,
Those who knew
Auschwitz, Bergen-Belzen,
Buchenwald, and
Who carry Holocaust memories,
Should understand oppression
And side with the oppressed.

January 2009

*(Israel's merciless bombing of Gaza
goes on as tanks destroy homes
and ceasefire proposals are ignored.)*

CLOSE THE PENTAGON!?

We speak glibly of wanting peace
And at Christmastime celebrate
"Peace on Earth, Goodwill to All."
Does "all"
Include our brothers and sisters
Around the world?

Can war's wasteful juggernaut
Be justified only for jobs and profits?
Year in and year out
Global corporations prosper
From death, destruction,
Lies, propaganda
And patriotic puffery
That lie at the heart of war
And "military preparedness."

Adults must solve problems as adults!
We must abandon war!

Who would not celebrate
The abandonment of wars,
A plague on mankind
Since long before long ago?

Who could object to:
 "No more killing and destruction!
No more finding new enemies!"
Who could object to
Finding peaceful resolutions

To inter-nation conflicts?

Who could object
To a "peace dividend"
From "no more war" spending
To benefit people everywhere?

Who, other than military brass
And countless corporations
Would not want to celebrate
The closing of the Pentagon?

Ah, but the repercussions
From dismantling the
Gargantuan centuries old
Self-perpetuating war industry?!
(A new "enemy" can always be found
To use devilish new war weapons,
The breath of perpetual wars.)

Is the war machine
"Too large to dismantle"?
....Millions unemployed and
Factories shuttered
Around the world?
With war abandoned,
Would the economy spiral downward
And become unhinged?

No!
New jobs would abound
As we repair the obsolescence
And decay that surround us

And produce necessities
For our neighbors on this planet?

But how then to use
The vacated Pentagon's massive obtuseness
And myriad corridors?

Could the Pentagon become
A vast hospital and rehab center
For wounded survivors of all wars,
From anywhere on Earth,
Even from former enemies?

With war abolished,
With the Department of Defense obsolete,
With the State Department reorganized,
Could the United States
Donate the Pentagon
To become headquarters for a new
Democratic Global Government?

Could the Pentagon thus become a
"Swords to plowshares" symbol –
A "huge step forward
From war and killing"
--For the human family"?

June 2009

HE SLIPPED AWAY TODAY

Brother Alan slipped away today.
His five years of travail…..
Auto accident, broken back,
Strokes, speech loss,
Little mobility…. are over.

Brilliant, inventive,
Non-combat veteran,
Always an activist,
Always a helping hand,
Always fun loving,
He is no longer with us,
Yet even in death
His body still serves.

After sixteen days of
Self-imposed denial,
Our brother enters family history,
His heaven - our memories.

*   *   *

Guard those memories tenderly
And help the young ones
Learn from his caring, his integrity,
His courage and his patience.

July 1, 2009

CHAPTER EIGHT – 2010S

SLAVES OF TIME?

Is each of us a slave of time?

We scurry here and there,
we hurry there and here
aware of schedules,
with calendar book
cell phone or clock in hand.

Within each human
is the deep pool of oneself….
strong-willed or weak,
outgoing, shy,
follower, leader,
artistic, creative…

Do clock-driven lives
devour or mask
our inner selves,
our true persona?
Is there a true persona
in there somewhere?

Do we run time pieces?
Do they run us?

November 2010

WIKILEAKS --
PENTAGON PAPERS of 2010?

In 1971
Daniel Ellsberg's "Pentagon Papers"
aroused the public and
helped a benumbed nation
extricate itself
from a decade-long,
diplomatically misguided
and tragic Vietnam quagmire.

Will Julian Assange's 2010 release
of secret State Department
and Pentagon messages and documents
- with thousands more to come –
awaken a recession-distracted
and bemused citizenry and
demystify the duplicity, foolishness,
deceits, insults, plots
and carelessness of so-called
"old fashioned diplomacy"?

State Department leaders should not
vilify and scapegoat Julian Assange.
They should thank him.
They should be embarrassed
at revealed epithets applied to leaders
around the world.

Can we do better? We must!

If we hope to find peace
in a turbulent, changing world
we must not remain
an arrogant rogue elephant
among the world's nations.
We must not ignore global
poverty and unrest
and needs of our own people,

Old fashioned diplomacy
in Latin America, the Near East
and elsewhere has failed us.
We have become bogged down
in wars of our own making
in Vietnam, Iraq and Afghanistan.
Yes, we CAN do better!

A new view of Mother Nature
and our neighbors
on this planet is needed!
A new cooperative,
diplomacy is needed!
War must be abandoned!
If we want peace,
fairness at home
and around the world
must become everyone's business!

We need more whistleblowers,

Carry on, Julian and Wikileaks!
Ignore legal machinations and
the noise of embarrassment
from Washington, D.C.

November 2010

(And we now have Manning and Snowden caught
in a similar "whistleblower" trap

THE CIRCLE OF CARING

When they are children
We teach them to care,
We teach them not to bully,
We teach them to love.

And then…..
An "enemy" is conjured,
A flag is waved
And grown children respond.

They are taught that
To kill is patriotic,
They must kill the "enemy."
And there is always an enemy....
With strange language,
With a different god,
With different skin color,
The enemy is not human.

So the circle of war goes on.
The circle of killing goes on.
The circle of hating goes on.
The circles of destruction
And waste
And futility
Go on.

The circle of caring is shattered.

The circles of cooperation
And humanity are broken,
Teachings of childhood: forgotten.

Only adults can break,
Only parents can break –
The vicious circle of war!

January 2011

FAMILY HISTORY?

A Viking broad sword, shield and helmet,
Deeply rusted, found on the Tuven farm.
They speak through many centuries,
Viking relics dug from poor farmland
On Glama's bend in Norway
Near King's Highway,
South of Elverum.

Before Ole Tuven unnumbered generations
Farmed the small farm,
Land so poor and so often flooded
That perhaps forebears
A millennia ago went on
Viking ventures to supplement
A meager living.

Or perhaps in a feudal age,
The Lokens and Kjeldes,
Wealthy lords
With Tuvens among their struggling serfs,
Forced their serfs
To partake in Viking ventures.

Ole Tuven, my grandfather,
Worked the small farm
On Glama's bend before
Purchasing or trading for

A small plot among Loken farms
To the west on Glama's floodplain,
Before migrating to the U.S. and Wisconsin.

Were some of my Viking forebears
"Terrorists" of a millennia ago,
As the world portrays them?
Or simple peasants
Struggling in an age when everywhere,
Even around the world,
Life was cheap and violence endemic?

May 2011

(On two or three occasions in talking with my Mother as a child, she spoke of her family coming from the bend in the Glama River a few miles south of Elverum in Norway, "not far from the King's Highway." She even drew two very rough sketches, which I still have. The Tuven and Loken farms were in that area. After Carol's and my tour of Norway with Jim Belgum's group in June 1994. I studied a Norwegian topographic map of the area and found notations of both the Loken and Tuven farms. I also found a symbol on the Tuven farm that Viking relics had been found buried there.)

DID WE DIE IN VAIN?
(Reflections of a Dead Soldier)

Since long before long ago
We have been wounded or killed
Just as we killed "enemies"
On countless battlefields.
By club, sword and spear,
In chariot-bowman battle,
In cavalry charge,
By musket, cannon and Gatling gun,
Rifle, machine gun,
Poison gas and biplane,
Dreadnaught, torpedo,
Aircraft carrier, roadside bomb,
And suicide bomber
The killing was done.

Death rained from above
By olive bomber and fighter plane,
Helicopter gunship, atom bomb,
Agent orange, napalm,
And lately by drone.

Since long before long ago
Many gave their lives,
Many more were grievously wounded,
For what?

Because oracle or shaman said
"The spirit says to kill enemies," or
A chief said "Protect our hunting ground,"
Or because king or pope said
"Take Jerusalem back from infidels!"
Or a president said "to save the Union,"
Or "This war will end all wars,"
Or "We must save the world for
democracy,"
Or "This is a 'good war' to end
Hitler, Mussolini and Tojo aggression,"
Or "This war is to end ethnic cleansing."

Our President now tells us,
"Support preemptive wars
Before the enemy attacks us!
Support us or you are an enemy!"

And now in non-wars (we are told) to
Kill shadowy terrorists.
We must oppose people's uprisings
(To feed our oil addiction,
As we turn a blind eye to other dictators
And coddle one "friendly" nation)?

War generates lies by friend and foe,
By dictator, ally or president...
An enemy can always be found,
With truth always war's first casualty.

Since long before long ago

Deaths on both sides lead to
More wars and more powerful
War machines raining violence,
Killing fathers, sons, brothers,
Sisters and mothers, infants,
Even from half-way around the globe,
Killing more senselessly
Than our early cousins,
To keep the "war industry humming"
And for "homeland security,"
As citizen rights and privacy dwindle.

Is there an answer?

When will adult men,
Turning from teenage macho
And fictional glory and "heroism,"
Learn that war solves no problem.
At war's end,
Victor and vanquished
Must meet around the same table
With old problems still there
And new ones looming.

Were our wounds and deaths in vain?
We still do not know.
We are waiting, yes, still waiting…
Our deaths and wounds
Are in limbo; we are still waiting.

We wait for the abandonment of war,
An end to the rapacious war industry.
We wait for a new beginning
Among the human family:
An era of cooperation, caring
And sharing Earth's limited resources.

Only then can our sacrifice be vindicated.
Only then can we know
Our deaths and wounds were NOT in vain.

June 5, 2011

*(This poem was written by a still-alive veteran.
Written on the day my older brother Edward died
at almost 92 years of age. My younger brother,
Alan, died in 2009 at 84, and I go on at 93. We
were all WWII veterans and, following my Dad's
strong beliefs about war, entered the war as non-
combat conscientious objectors (an approved
category during World War II when about 90% of
all servicemen and women were "non-combat.").
Very fortunately, each of us learned a lot and
suffered no injury. Ed served in Europe with
Patton's 3rd army, Al in the South Pacific and I in
West and North Africa.)*

CHAPTER NINE - EPILOGUE

Family

GRIEVE NOT FOR ME

Grieve not long when my days are done,
I'm family rich; the world I've seen,
With loved ones I have shared my years.
So when I'm gone please shed few tears.

I tried good to do along the way
And spread some cheer to brighten days.
My days were full, my turn was long!
So celebrate when I am gone!

October 1996

ALPHABETICAL LIST OF POEMS

POEMS BY TOPICAL GROUPS
(Several poems are in more than one group.)

FAMILY
Christy is My Dad
Family History?
Grieve Not For Me
He Slipped Away Today
I Love You
Our Mother
September 5, 1939
Sparkle Eyes

NATURE
Ghost Ship
Gold Tatters
Moments of Peace
New Beginnings
Point of View
Savanna
To a Day Lily Stalk

PHILOSPOHY/PERSPECTIVE
Campfire
Freedom
Give Yourself the Present
Point of view
The People Are America
Threads of Consciousness

RECORD/HISTORY
China 1987
Common Sense Tells Us
Did We Die I Vain?
The Dragon's New Coat
Family History
Of, By and For the Few
Washington After Hours
Wikileaks
Wilike Morning

RELIGIOUS
Amazing Love
Dust in the Sunlight
God and the Blind Men
In Whose Image?
The Spirits of Christmas
Thou Shalt Not Kill

TRAVEL
China 1987
Forgotten Night
Green Hair
The Dragons New Coat
Savanna
Wilike Morning

WAR

WHIMSY

MISCELLANEOUS

www.ingramcontent.com/pod-product-compliance
Lightning Source LLC
Chambersburg PA
CBHW051841040426
42447CB00006B/638